A wise man once told ... *was...*

If Offered a Mint, Take It.

Dan De Kalb
© 2015

For Courtney and Creighton…
The two best friends I've ever helped make.

Let me know if you have questions!

Introduction

For my two children who I love more than I can describe:

I am convinced that everyone must know during their lifetime (to varying degrees) how to own, operate, manage, work at, and at the very least survive in some type of business environment. At some point in your life, you will be an employee, coworker, manager, supervisor, director, president, CEO, and possibly even an owner. Although most formal educations include some type of "business" course requirement, these often focus on areas such as economics, finance, accounting, or statistics, and do not delve very deeply into how to get through to quitting time without strangling a supervisor, coworker, employee, customer, or the receptionist at the front desk. The ability to do so is normally part of "on-the-job-training," and is often learned in the "School of Hard Knocks" rather than the College of Business. The following is my attempt to share opinions, advice, and anecdotes on business that are based on things I've seen, heard, and read, as well as my firsthand experiences. I'm doing this so that you may have a jumpstart on the learning curve and not duplicate my mistakes.

Four years ago, my daughter graduated high school and left for college. At the same time, my son was just beginning high school. I figured that four years later one would be going to college and the other would either be continuing her education or entering the job market. At that time, I began planning what I could do to help them in their endeavors. I offered this to them in celebration of their respective graduations from college and high school in the spring of 2015.

Don't get stressed if you can't get a room full of engineers to agree.

Present a problem to a room of ten engineers and you will likely get ten different solutions. There may be a chance that you will get nine solutions due to the possibility that two of the engineers will actually agree. Likewise, you may receive more than ten solutions when at least one engineer is unable to decide on a "best" solution and provides you with an alternative. This is acceptable, and should be anticipated, as engineers are not the most decisive group of individuals. The situation may worsen if the remaining nine engineers discover one of their cohorts provided you with an alternate. This will, in turn, open the floodgates since those nine (not to be outdone) will begin providing their own alternate solutions. Engineers may not be the most decisive group of individuals, but their indecisiveness pales in comparison to their competitiveness.

Carefully consider what management (really) expects you to do.

When you are given a level of authority and are tasked to provide solutions within that authority, management expects you to provide solutions. However, you must consider whether management will judge you for providing solutions within your authority, or whether they will allow you to provide solutions that are beyond your authority. Ask yourself, "What will impress management more: telling people what they must do because you have the authority, or providing a solution based on having led people to a desired outcome?"

Do not expect a diverse group to decide by consensus.

It is important to have diversity in every group if you want multiple opinions and perspectives. However, the more diversity you have in a group, the less chance there is that everyone will agree on anything. The problem with deciding by consensus is that every individual has veto power. Consequently, a diverse group will never get anything meaningful accomplished deciding by consensus because a compromise will be required. This is not necessarily a bad thing. You must simply weigh the importance of and prioritize decision-making policies versus diversity when assembling a group of individuals.

When dealt with a setback, you have two options.
You can use it as an excuse, or you can use it as motivation.

Use every failure as a learning experience. Determine what went wrong and change the process. Set a new goal and strive to move forward again. I do not know of anyone who achieved true, long-term success by relying on excuses. Never forget the setbacks and use them as motivation.

The only advantage of putting the cart in front of the horse is that you no longer have to look at the horse's ass.

When you embark on a project, you must establish priorities, requirements, and prerequisites. Analyze them and then map out your strategy. Do not jump to conclusions. Never assume and always have a plan. Once you decide on the plan, stick to it until the wheels come flying off the cart. At that time leave the cart behind, get on the horse, and go find a new cart.

Do not fear a well-earned ego.

Do actions really speak louder than words? At what point must you speak up to ensure your audience is getting the message? Regardless of how much effort you put forth, you may go unnoticed because your audience was not aware of your actions because you were relying on them to get you noticed rather than your words. Everyone gets annoyed by the person who is always the first one to raise their hand. However, there are times when you need to speak up to be heard; it may be in your best interest as well as the best interest of the group. The key is to walk a fine line between humility and pride and make choices that maximize your chances of successfully reaching your goals. There are times for humility and there are times for pride. The challenge is to determine which time is which based on your goals and your audience. There is no embarrassment in knowing the answer and being the most informed in the room. However, there is embarrassment when the project fails because you didn't contribute when you knew you had the answer. Occasionally you have to stop sitting on your hands and raise one of them to be noticed, but be sure to alternate hands so that one is always warm.

No one ever won by doing exactly what their competition did.

Very few businesses go to market without a competitor. Business is a competitive business. Success is achieved because you perform better than your competition. Companies often choose to enter an existing market and attempt to copy the market leader. Instead, they should change the rules and do something different than what the leader is already doing and doing quite successfully. The market leader is leading for all the obvious reasons. They have already optimized their product and processes. Even more so, they already have experience in the market that they are competing in. To beat the competition, you have to be better than them, not equal to them. Imitation may be the sincerest form of flattery, but you do not want to flatter your competition, you want to beat them.

Who's the most successful organization in the market?
It's the one everyone is criticizing.

In the rare case that your strengths are somehow identical in every way to your competition's, you must determine your critical strength and then raise it to a new level. Rather than criticizing your competition, work to outperform them. There is always room for improvement. The key is to determine your strengths and improve those that can give you the best return and ultimately a competitive edge. Take note of which competitor everyone is talking about. Chances are that they are the leader and the one that represents the greatest threat to your success. There's no benefit in criticizing the competitors that are lagging behind since they offer no threat, and comparing yourself to them does no good. Find out who the leading competitor in your industry is, and use them as the benchmark of where you need to be performing above.

Never rely on checking the output to guarantee its quality.

Most processes generally take an input and create an output. A substantial amount of effort is placed on measuring and reporting the quality of the output since it is the output that the customer receives and since quality is one of the three essential keys to success (the other two being price and service). However, in an effort to ensure quality, the output often receives too much attention. The question you must consider is, "How much checking and reviewing is needed?" If you rely on the review to catch errors and you still have quality issues, do you invest in a second round of reviews? What guarantee do you have that the second review will catch all of the errors if the first review didn't?

Computer programmers like to say, "garbage in, garbage out," indicating that the output will only ever be as good as the input. They are, of course, assuming that the processes they programmed work flawlessly and that the quality issues are a result of the input. Their pride in ownership prevents them from admitting that the error may be in the process as well as the input. They are only half correct with this statement since flawless man-made processes are extremely rare. Given that fact, you cannot "check-in" quality by focusing on the output. You will never have enough resources to review it enough times. You must build tested quality into the process and then invest time in checking the input. Until you do so, you will always have to review the output (and listen to the programmers brag about their programming prowess).

There's no need to prescribe an aspirin if the patient has a hatchet in the back of their head.

Issues will arise that require your attention, and it will be vitally important to determine and differentiate the symptoms versus the cause of the issue. The symptom is often just an indication that there is a problem, but inevitably it gets more than its fair share of attention. Use the symptoms to help determine the cause, but don't accept one for the other. Experts will tell you to "drill down to determine the root cause" or "peel back the layers of the onion." Others believe that you must reply "Why" to a minimum of five subsequent responses before you can determine the true cause of an issue. There's no set rule that will apply to every case, you just have to analyze the situation, determine the difference between the symptoms and the causes and be careful that you are treating the cause, not the symptom.

If 90% accuracy is acceptable for you,
is it acceptable for everyone else in your organization?

We are taught that 90% accuracy will get us an "A" grade. That may sound acceptable, but consider it from your customer's perspective. If you perform at 90%, one out of ten of your customers is going to receive a flawed product or service. Before you decide this is acceptable, I suggest you survey your customers and inquire which one out of ten is willing to accept the flawed product or service. I doubt you will get 10% to volunteer. To make matters worse, if your process is part of a system of multiple processes, you must consider if it is acceptable for everyone to operate at 90% accuracy. Consider a system with 5 steps that all operate at 90% accuracy. The final product could have an accuracy level as low as:
90%*90%*90%*90%*90%= 59%.
Is this acceptable? If so, you will need to find 4 of those 10 customers to accept a flawed product or service. Good luck with that! Let me know how it works for you!

The more times you run over a speed bump,
the more it is worn down.
Eventually, it is no longer a speed bump.

There will always be obstacles along the way. They will come in every shape and size, and they will occur when you least expect them. The key to success depends on how you deal with them. Few obstacles are insurmountable. And in case they are, you must develop a strategy to acknowledge them and work your way around them. Far more often, you can develop a strategy to deal with them in a way that they are even less of an obstacle the next time you encounter them. Eventually, your strategies will be such that what was once an obstacle will be worn smooth. Just don't tell the city streets department about it.

If offered a mint…take it.

This is self-explanatory, and no commentary is required.

Be more than a valuable employee.
Be an invaluable employee.

There will come a time when the business environment will require management to look at the workforce and determine who they need to part ways with and who they need to keep on staff in order to operate more efficiently. As cold as it may seem, management will review each employee and rank them (figuratively and/or literally) based on their contribution. Note that unless they own the company, managers are employees as well and this process will be applied to all levels within the organization. At times like this, it is important to remember that a manager's primary goal is not to reward employees for high performance; it is their goal to stay in business. The employees most likely to be retained are the employees that management cannot survive without, and these are not necessarily the employees who work the hardest. This is not to discourage hard work, quite the contrary. An employee should contribute to the organization's success to the point where management recognizes that its future success depends on that employee. In the event of organizational downsizing, never settle on being "just grateful to have a job when the dust settles," but instead be the one that management is "grateful to have on staff."

Always take the high road.
The view is much better.

Regardless of your position in the organization, your comments about others say everything about you, so strive to be positive. There will be countless opportunities when your input is requested, and it may be challenging to find something nice to say or offer a compliment. This doesn't require you to be insincere or even lie. You can offer criticism as long as it is constructive and not personal. Remember that everything you put forth reflects back upon you, and you will want that reflection to leave you in the best possible light.

Your customers don't need to know what your cost is.
They need only know what their price is.

Unless you are a nonprofit organization, the price at which you provide a product or service can most easily be represented by the following equation:

Price = Total Cost + Profit

While you are the one who ultimately decides the amount of profit you plan to have, you can control only certain parts of what goes into your total cost while you have even less control, if any at all, of what the market dictates the price must be for you to compete. Determine what your customer's price must be in order for you to compete, determine what your costs are, and then calculate your profit by rearranging the above equation to be:

Profit = Price – Total Cost

Then if you decide you are unsatisfied with the amount of profit, you can increase the price and risk being uncompetitive. The more challenging action is to reduce your cost and, by doing so, maintain your price or reduce your price with the possibility of increasing your competitiveness and, in turn, increase your profit. You must keep in mind that your customer has their own motives, interests, and desires to be competitive in their respective market. If you inform them of your costs, they can calculate your profit because they already know the price. Your price is your customer's cost. As you are working to reduce your costs, so are they. Don't let them reduce their cost by knowing enough to reduce your profit.

Leadership is pulling rather than pushing.

No great leader became so from the back of the pack. To be a leader you must be out front setting an example for others to follow while establishing expectations through your words and actions. You must put yourself on the line while at the same time placing others first. By "first", I do not mean first in line to absorb the hits for you. I mean to lift them up and hold their wellbeing and success as your primary goal. Your success depends on their success, and their success depends on yours. Create that relationship and lead from the front but be sure to be back among your troops before dark or risk being shot by your own men.

Never travel in clothes that are inappropriate for your first appointment.
Assume the airline is going to lose you baggage.

A friend was flying from his divisional headquarter's hometown to his first meeting at the new corporate headquarters. Since he could not be late, he scheduled himself to be on the first flight leaving in the morning, arriving at noon, with ample time to check in to the hotel, get refreshed, and be at his 3:30 meeting with the corporate management. He chose to dress as casual as possible that morning wearing shorts, flip flops, and a bright Hawaiian shirt in order to be relaxed on the flight, and planned to change into his suit at the hotel prior to his meeting. He arrived on schedule but his baggage did not. He was assured that his bags were on the next flight which would land a couple hours later and still in time for him to change and make his meeting. When the next flight arrived, he was at baggage claim but his baggage was not. By then he had just enough time to make it to the meeting, which he rushed to in his shorts, flip flops, and bright Hawaiian shirt. This may have not been an issue, and he may have made an incredible first impression if he was working for a surfboard manufacturer. He was not.

Pack with the intent of coordinating all clothes to work with the same belt and shoes.

If you are travelling on a multiday business trip and plan to see the same people over that time, they may notice if you wear the same clothes every day, particularly once your clothes become dirty and smelly. However, unless you work in the clothing or fashion industry, your associates will not notice or care if you wear the same shoes and belt every day. You can reduce your packing requirements by coordinating all of your clothes to look good with the same belt and shoes.

The first word in "business dinner" is "business".

You don't go to a business dinner to eat, so watch what you eat. If you are on the receiving end of the invitation, follow your host's lead. Consider what you order, and the chances you will spill, splatter, or drip. Consider how often you will be wiping your hands and mouth before you decide what food you will be ordering. Monitor your portion size and the amount of your conversation so that you are neither the first nor the last to finish, assuming there are more than two sharing the meal. In only rare cases, you should lick your fingers, and in all cases order water to drink initially and wait to see what your host has to drink. The same rules apply if you are the one offering the invitation. But in that case, take note if your guest follows any of the above tips.

Elaborate only when asked to, and stick to the topic.

Keep your answers short and to the point. If the boss wants you to elaborate, he will ask you to. Stay on topic. Monitor the conversation topic. You must follow the boss when he changes the topic. If there is more to offer on the previous topic, you can follow up later. Keep track of who is driving the conversation. Unless it is you, you are along for the ride and must not be a backseat driver. Keep professional conversations professional. Do not show pictures of your kids or discuss your hobbies in the board room. If the boss is interested, he will invite you to a conversation at a less formal location. Even then, be aware of why you are invited into a conversation. Does the boss want to talk business or get to know you personally? If you are the boss, be sure to know who follows these rules. If you choose to tolerate those who don't, schedule your conversations accordingly.

Do not whisper in a crowd.

Do not bring up a topic in conversation that you do not want everyone to hear. Take the sidebar conversation outside or have it at a later date. Do not refer to something that may be of interest to everyone in the room unless you plan to share with everyone. It is rude to refer to a topic with a member of the crowd unless everyone in the crowd knows what you are referring to. It is even ruder to point out that you plan to have the private conversation with select members of the group since the others know about it now. If they do not need to be included, it is best if they are unaware that they are not included.

A 50% reduction requires a 100% increase in order to recover.
Wow! Really?

Statistics are essential in tracking performance, but you must be careful in how they are used and what type you use. Applying percentages or ratios can often be misleading. You must decide when they are appropriate versus when using the raw numbers are appropriate. It depends on the message you are needing and able to convey.

If you plan to be outstanding in your field,
be prepared for all types of weather.

Whether you are an overachiever, high performer, or just someone who is willing to go out on a limb to excel, you must be prepared for exposure. Business is a competitive business. Work to be the best at what you choose to do and know that your friends will support you while others may resent, ridicule, or criticize you in order to pull you back to their level. It's their way of competing and making up for their lack of success. Don't take it personally. As long as you come by your success through honesty and hard work, never let their disappointments keep you from excelling. The taller you stand, the more of a lightning rod you become. But don't worry; your chances of being run over in the crosswalk are still greater.

People do not know what they do not know.

Too many people claim to know what others need, think, and feel. If they could read the minds of others, they could earn a fortune. There's a reason why you find mind readers and fortune tellers working in dilapidated structures in undesirable neighborhoods near the airport. The first step in training, teaching, or mentoring is to acknowledge that you do not know what the pupil knows and doesn't know. The next step is to try and learn what they know and don't know. They will know what they know and they will gladly tell you so. You will know what they know they do not know when they ask you to tell them so. But the only way to determine what they do not know that they do not know is for you to ask them so. Only when you learn what they know and do not know can you determine what they need to know and what bit of knowledge you need to share with them, assuming you know it.

The three primary components of a project are:
scope, schedule, and resources.

Many projects begin with a great idea and a defined scope. In other words, someone has determined what the project is intended to accomplish, and they go to management with great news of a proposal. A schedule is created next wherein someone determines when the project will be completed. Finally, the resources are determined and everyone at that point knows how much money, people, raw materials, etc. are required to commit to the project. If you are lucky, very lucky (noting that I do not believe in luck), the available resources will be sufficient to fulfill the scope of the project within the scheduled time. This never happens.

Someone will point out that the available resources are not adequate to fill the scope and you must add resources. Someone else will point out that even if the resources were adequate the scope could never be filled within schedule, and the project will require more time. Someone else will point out that you have no additional resources to add and that the time is critical so the scope must be reduced and management will not get the end result they were promised. At this point, no one will volunteer to present the bad news to management.

Begin your projects by determining which of the three components are not variable, and then determine how much of the variable components you require to accomplish the project. If the scope, schedule, or resource has to vary, then determine how much they will change and redefine them before proposing it to management. If management comes to you with a project, request details on all three components, and don't be surprised if they have unrealistic expectations for one or more.

*If approached by a stranger asking your name,
do not tell them but, instead, ask them why they want to know. They
may be serving a subpoena.*

If you have to ask me why I suggest this, then you probably don't have anything to worry about and can go ahead and tell them your name. They may be an old acquaintance.

Figures never lie but liars figure.

My engineering statistics professor was fond of pointing this out. Statistics are very important tools to support an argument. You should exercise caution with people who repeatedly cite statistics. Ask to see the raw data AND find out how much of it was used to create the statistics being cited. The key here is "how much of it." There is always enough raw data available to create a statistic that will support just about any agenda a person is putting forth. Likewise, it is helpful to remember this when you have your own agenda to put forth. For specific examples, study political campaign speeches.

If you can't measure it,
it doesn't exist.

Consequently, everything is measurable. Organizational success is composed of countless factors all working together towards a common goal. Some of these are very tangible while others are not so. Some can be reviewed very objectively while others require a more subjective approach. Case in point, you can measure an employee's quality and productivity by looking directly at their output and comparing it to the expectations you have placed on that employee. But how do you measure something like job satisfaction or morale? Ineffective managers will place these types of items under the "unmeasurable" or "subjective" category, move on, and not give them enough attention. Optimize your organization's performance by recognizing that its optimal success depends on ALL factors working together. You may not be able to assign a hard metric to all factors, but if you dig deep enough you will find that those items hard to measure subjectively have an impact on items measured objectively. This means that those subjective items can, in fact, be measured. Case in point, you may not be able to place a value on job satisfaction but it, along with other factors, has a direct impact on quality (which is easily measured). The key here is to never disregard something because it is difficult to measure. If it has impact, look at what it impacts and measure the impact instead. Measure the symptom if you can't measure the cause, and this may help you determine the cause. Everything is measurable.

Don't get caught in an organizational chart that is too vertical or too horizontal.

Some type of organizational hierarchy will exist once the organization grows larger than one person. Many organizations illustrate their internal hierarchy with a chart that indicates who reports to whom and how the departments interrelate. Names are placed in boxes with lines connecting employees and their supervisors. The org chart will appear to be "vertical" when the organization has multiple layers in the reporting structure and few people at each layer. Likewise, it will appear "horizontal" when there are few layers in the reporting structure and many people at each layer. You must know where you are on the chart and how the chart is aligned if you have a desire to increase your level of responsibility, receive a promotion, and "move up" in the chart. The downside of being in a vertical org chart is that you have few reporting to you while there are few reporting to your supervisor. If you only have one person reporting to you, and you are the only person reporting to your supervisor, intelligent management will question what your level of responsibility brings to the company. Can your employee report to your supervisor and, if so, why do they need you? The downside of a horizontal org chart is that you may have too many people to effectively supervise while there may be too many people reporting to your supervisor. Remember that these people at your level on the chart reporting to your supervisor represent possible competition, assuming you desire to move up the chart into your supervisor's position.

Words mean things.

Never underestimate the importance of what people say. Likewise, what you say reflects directly upon you. I once had a manager who repeatedly reminded me of what I had earlier said and held me to it. I pointed this out to him and he denied having said anything.

Surround yourself with honest positive people.

There is plenty of negativity in the world. When you associate with the pessimists, cynics, and naysayers, you risk being drug down through "guilt by association" within the organization. You will get more accomplished by teaming with positive people who are honest and sincere in their outlook. Find coworkers and employees who will provide sincere input and feedback. Good leaders know deep down that they are good leaders and do not need a bunch of "yes" men to prop them up into their leadership positions. They do not need to surround themselves with crowds to be reminded how great they are. Leaders who search for and accept hollow compliments will eventually report to work in the nude someday.

Dress for your next position.

Never be satisfied with the status quo. You should always strive for something better. When you set your sights on your next position, part of your plan should be to envision what it requires, what it offers, and what you like about that position. Make it easier for others to share that same vision with you by looking the part. One of the people to share the vision may be the person with the authority to help you make it happen. Dressing for it will make it easier for them to see you in it.

Never be afraid to train your replacement.
You are more likely to be promoted if you can be replaced.

Bring value to the organization and your position is more secure. Bring enough value to the organization for smart management to recognize it, and they will provide you with more opportunities for responsibility and advancement. Once you advance, management (and very possibly you) will need to find someone to fill the void that your advancement created. The easier this is to do, the more likely management will provide you with the advancement. One of the first things you should do in any position is to develop a succession plan for all of your employees as well as yourself. With regards to your employees, you should be prepared if one or more of them are no longer available to fulfill their responsibilities. You should expect that your manager has already done the same. There are those who will argue that once you train your replacement you will be replaced, implying that you will be left out. I disagree. An employee that is invaluable to the success of the organization never has to be concerned that they will be left out. Smart management knows the company's success depends on an invaluable employee and so should you.

Terminating someone's employment should not be fun.

If you are tasked with terminating another employee's position, take a moment and think back over their career. Did you recruit them? If so, what did you see in them that convinced you they would be an asset? Was it not there? If it wasn't, why did you think it was? Did you hire them? Remember how excited you were about them joining your organization. They were more than likely excited about it as well. If you were not excited, why did you hire them? Did you train them? If they cannot perform their responsibilities, did you train them properly? If they are incapable of being trained for the job, why didn't you know this before you hired them? Did you expect them to succeed? If so, did you give them every opportunity and tool they needed? If not, why did you waste your time, their time, and the organization's resources? Are you simply "trimming fat", cutting back the "dead wood", or parting ways with "under performers"? If so, ask yourself why you overstaffed, paid people for not working, or permitted expectations not to be met.

I knew a manager who once stated that he had to hire ten people to find one good one. I believe it was his ability to recruit and hire that was flawed. I sat at a business dinner one night listening to other managers gloat while they reminisced on their favorite stories of how they "got to fire some guy". I excused myself from dinner, which was a shame since it was a really good steakhouse.

The people you recruit, hire, and train are a direct reflection on you and a major investment for the organization. Rejoice when you are able to offer someone an opportunity. If they fail, be cautious. Their failure may be yours.

Your success depends upon not only those you work for, but also those who work for you.

Unless you are the owner or an entry-level employee, you will be in a position that has responsible charge of some of your coworkers while at the same time being accountable to others. Consider the organization to be a team that is only as strong as its weakest member. When your employees succeed, you succeed, give them every opportunity to do so. When your supervisor succeeds, you succeed, so do everything you can to work for their success.

Know how to do your job.
Know how to do your employee's job.
Know how to do your boss's job.

It goes without saying that you must be capable of filling the expectations placed on you and your position. If not, you are wasting your time and you should either request additional training or find a different job. There are advantages to knowing how to perform the tasks you assign to others in that you have a better understanding of what is possible and what you can expect. It may not be required in all cases, since it is their responsibility and not yours, but you must at least have a basic understanding of their job requirements in order to manage them effectively. In many organizations, employee advancement is typically characterized by the employee moving into the manager's position. Your chances of being chosen for advancement will improve if you already know how to do your boss's job. Restrain your actions and words if you realize you can do your boss's job better than your boss can. The boss may not be receptive, and your chances of being chosen for advancement may decrease especially if your boss is on the selection committee.

Say what you are going to do, and then do what you said you were going to do.

It's all about credibility. There is an obvious disadvantage to "overpromising and underdelivering". You will not enjoy any type of success by falling short of what you have committed to do. Many people subscribe to the practice of "underpromising and overdelivering", but I believe that any type of success enjoyed as a result of this type of commitment will be short lived. Continuing this practice will result in your customers beginning to expect it and then your commitment is no longer valid and you will set yourself up for failure the first time you do not deliver more than you promised. Even worse, your "underpromise" may be such that it fails to meet your customers' expectation and you never get the opportunity to deliver. You may not be able to deliver on every promise you make and, if not, you must explain your failure to your customer. But do not set yourself up for failure by promising more than you can deliver or purposely promising less than you can deliver.

You should question the honesty of a person who starts a sentence, "To be honest with you…"

If a person feels the need to begin a conversation by prefacing their statement and reminding you that they are not lying, you should question how honest they were when they did not go to those lengths to preface their statement and remind you of how honest they were. Some will use this phrase in order to emphasize the importance of a statement. The fastest way to get them to discontinue is to ask them if they were being honest when not using the phrase.

If the phone rings, answer it.

Whether in business or not, always answer the phone. It may be an emergency. It may be an offer for the opportunity of a lifetime. It may be a telemarketer and you can unload the stress of your day on them (unless they're selling something really cool).

The customer is NOT always right,
and it's your job to prevent the customer from discovering that fact.

The customer/provider relationship is just that. It's a relationship. In all relationships there is give and take. However, in this relationship, the provider's success almost always depends on the customer's satisfaction. And face it, everyone feels satisfied when they are convinced they are right. The key here is that they need to be convinced they are right so that they are satisfied, and you must help with this since it is in your best interest as a provider. Losing customers is costly. It requires a substantial resource investment to replace them. Never lie to them, but foster a relationship where your customer is convinced they are right and satisfied and your chances of having a repeat customer will improve. They can be as wrong as all get-out, but don't dare tell them. After all, they are the customer, and as the experts say, "The customer's always right."

Nothing good ever happens after the third drink.

I was always told that nothing ever good happens after midnight, but then I got a summer job working third shift in a factory. Good things happened for me. I worked hard, produced an efficient quality product, made enough money to return to school, and never worked third shift again. So I will modify that statement to address alcohol and business. Unless you work for a business that buys, sells, or produces alcohol, never mix alcohol with business. It's as simple as that. I have seen good careers destroyed by alcohol. Mean people get meaner when they drink. Dumb people get dumber when they drink. Funny people convince themselves that they get funnier when they drink. But have you ever noticed that smart people do not get smarter when they drink, and the really smart ones don't mix drink with business?

Gravity is your friend.
Don't fight it.
Instead, use it to your advantage.

There are very few constants. But when something is proven to be constant, it becomes dependable. When it becomes completely dependable, it becomes predictable. And when it becomes predictable, you should use it to your advantage. There is no more dependable, constant force on earth than gravity. It could be argued that peer pressure is a close second but, technically, it is a pressure and not a force. Design every process, procedure, tool, and system to include and capitalize on the existence of gravity. Use it to your advantage since it is predictable, dependable, and constant.

Once a thought leaves your brain, it is public domain.

There is no privacy left in the world outside of your own mind. Once your thoughts are spoken, written, or acted upon they are available for the world to know. It doesn't matter whether you share them during or after work hours. There is no virtual time clock that prevents them from showing up at work tomorrow (with or without you).

The surest way to prevent getting caught doing something wrong is to not do something wrong.

Temptations come in every shape and size and will appear when you least expect them. There are consequences to your actions, and you must decide whether you want to pay those consequences or receive payment for them. There is no perfect crime.

Attitude is contagious.
You can catch it just as easily as you can share it.

This applies to a good attitude as well as a bad attitude, so you should always be positive. You will see setbacks, bad days, and times when things aren't going the way you would like them to, but get over it. That's all part of life. The key is how you react to them. Every office will have its share of attitudes that run the full gamut. Management knows which employees bring a positive attitude to work every day just as employees know which managers bring one. You will get more accomplished and achieve more success with a positive attitude.

The more you have, the more you have to lose.

You will make wise decisions as time goes on, and those decisions will lead to successes. Of this, I have no doubt. Always appreciate what you have achieved and know that it is only temporary. Generations have labored in countless ways to provide you the opportunities you have. Be thankful and show your gratitude by providing similar opportunities for others.

Success is providing solutions that others couldn't (or just didn't).

Countless individuals have enjoyed successful careers providing solutions that others couldn't provide. Business is all about providing solutions, and solutions are as varied as the problems they solve. Develop a systematic approach to problem solving that works for you and make it broad enough that you can apply it to every problem. I have seen many approaches and have tried almost as many. Ultimately, I combined the aspects of several to get to one that works for me. It goes as follows:

1. Determine the symptoms, and do not rush to accept the symptoms as the actual problem that needs solving.
2. Analyze the symptoms until you determine what the problem is.
3. Once you have determined the problem, determine the intent and requirements of the solution.
4. Create a list of possible solutions knowing that there may be many.
5. Rank your list of possible solutions based on your priorities whether it be cost, ease, timing, etc.
6. Make a choice as to which solution you will use. Be decisive. It will be obvious in time whether you made the right decision.
7. Proceed with your choice and implement it.
8. Determine the impact and acceptability of your solution. You may have to wait a while, but include a time limit as part of the solution.
9. Decide whether the problem was solved. If not, review your notes and determine how far back up this list you need to go and start again. Don't be afraid to go all the way back to the first step since you should have learned something during this process and are now more informed.

Change is good unless it is for the sake of change.

Humans are creatures of habit, and they do things the way they do because they are comfortable in doing them that way. Whether they receive tangible rewards, a sense of accomplishment, or satisfaction of some type, it all boils down to their desire to be comfortable. Most have developed their own specific comfort zone, and they do not care to step out of it. For this reason, change does not come easy or natural for some, and is resisted at all costs by others. The business world is not static, and organizations require ongoing change to remain competitive. History is littered with people, organizations, and industries that failed to change and then failed all together. However, change is only good if it is required, and it is not always required. Your opportunity as an employee is to recognize the need and subsequent benefits of change and then embrace it, while your opportunity as a manager is to ensure that your employee does so.

What do you do when the boss says,
"I'd rather you ask for forgiveness than ask for permission."

You will encounter more management styles than you do managers since most managers, especially the good ones, will change their approach over time as their job expectations change. Some you will like, and some you will not. This is inevitable in the same way that not everyone you manage will agree with your style of management. You will have some managers who make their expectations very clear and others who do not. The latter case is more difficult while they may know what their expectations are, but just don't communicate them well enough to be obvious. You will encounter micromanagers who give you absolutely no latitude, show no apparent faith in you, and who down deeply desire to be doing your job instead of theirs. You will encounter absentee managers who give you no direction and then criticize you for not meeting their expectations, quite obviously assuming that you can read minds. But there is one manager who is either the laziest, the trickiest, or quite possibly the best of all. The manager who does not intend to communicate until you fail may do so because they know nothing about your job and have no desire to know. They might do so to set you up for failure, which is not good for either you or the manager, they might do so to determine how much initiative you will take. This would be a great opportunity for you. This manager is giving you full responsibility while also holding you accountable. They are hinting they will accept your failures but do not intend to be held accountable for them. They do this by suggesting you ask for your own forgiveness. This can be a win-win management style for the manager and you. Take this opportunity and run with it but be cautious. If the manager is a good manager, they will realize that their success depends on your success and will understand if you ask for permission. But do so only after you have exhausted your other options.

Employees are more likely to "buy-in"
if you give them ownership of what they purchase.

Everyone who actively participates in a decision-making process has ownership in the decision. Whether they agreed to it or not, they had the opportunity to provide input and contribute to the outcome. Whether they agreed to it or not, they should come away from the process understanding the decision and the basis on which it was reached. Decisions have impact, and the impact may be far reaching throughout your department, division and organization. As a manager it will be your responsibility in many cases to explain and implement the decision and the changes that are required. Do not be surprised if you are met with questions and resistance particularly if the decision results in a change for your employees. The fastest way to get the affected parties to accept the change is to ensure that they were included in the decision to change. It may be impossible to include others, and it may be impractical to give everyone a vote or a "place at the table". Your communication and management ability is tested during this phase. Decide what level of influence you can allow others to have on the decision and how their input is best utilized, then let them know it is. A good employee will understand that they have limited input but will appreciate the opportunity to provide, and they will be more receptive to the outcome.

If you dread going to work in the morning,
imagine how much worse it will be when you have to work alongside
an ex-lover.

Romance and business do not mix. Never start a romantic relationship with a coworker. Never, ever start a romantic relationship with an employee. And never, ever, ever start a romantic relationship with your boss (unless you want their job and in that case plan ahead to have undisputable evidence of the relationship).

Develop a set of mutual expectations between employees and managers.

Regardless of what side of the desk you are sitting, communication goes both ways. As an employee you need to know what management expects of you. You will not succeed until you fully know, understand, and accept these expectations. Likewise, as a manager, you must be sure that your expectations are adequately communicated and understood by your employees; otherwise, you cannot rightly hold them accountable. There is one more step in this that many overlook. As a manager you should ask your employee what they expect of you. Those who disagree with this normally fail as managers. Do not hesitate to ask your employees what they expect of you. You can learn a lot about them from their response. You may learn something new. Once you learn what their expectations are, be honest about the potential of you being able to meet those expectations. Make sure they understand what they can expect from you, and they will be more likely to meet or exceed the expectations you have placed on them.

The key to business success is a three-legged stool: price, quality, and service.
Without all three legs, the stool will collapse and you will fall on your ass.

Business success is defined by converting an input into an output and providing a quality output to a customer at a competitive price greater than your cost. This applies regardless of the output you are selling, and the goal is the same whether it is a product or service. There are organizations that focus specifically on price and being the "low-price leader". They do not focus on quality or service. If you choose to do this, you will sell large quantities, but you must have a lot of customers since the amount of profit per customer will be driven down due to the low price. There are organizations that focus their efforts on quality. The advantage of doing this is that customers will pay more for the additional quality but you will not sell as many units. Finally, there are organizations that choose to focus on service allowing them to get a slightly higher price and provide average quality. The customer may pay a bit more and not worry about quality if they feel they are being treated better than normal while doing so. Many organizations have failed because they placed too much emphasis on one of these factors while neglecting the other two. Successful companies have determined the right combination of the three for the market they have chosen to serve. In doing so, they will remain successful only if they continue to monitor the market's demand. A three-legged stool will not wobble regardless of the surface you place it one. You can level that stool out perfectly and enjoy your success if you adjust each leg to the proper length.

The receptionist may hold the keys to the executive washroom.

Learn how your organization operates and what members of the organization play the largest role in its success. Don't be surprised to learn that customers return because of a friendly receptionist, clean forks, an attractive website, a secure parking lot, or any number of things that are the direct responsibility and result of an employee going above and beyond their job description. Whether they know it or not, they are more than a valuable employee. They have become an invaluable employee. They may not know it, but smart management knows it and smart management knows who they are. If they are so valuable, why are they not in management? A valuable employee, and even an invaluable employee, may not necessarily be a good manager. They may not have the right skill set or the aspiration to be in management, and good management will know this. You need to know who these people are, making sure they know you and strive to become one of them. They have the attention and the "ear" of management. Management knows who they are and management listens to them. Management will listen to you as well, if you are one of them

A pat on the back will push an employee
further than a kick in the pants.
It's simple physics.

No one is perfect. Everyone makes mistakes. The key is to learn from the mistakes and not repeat them. If an employee is unaware they have made a mistake, it is management's responsibility to inform them, take the appropriate actions, and help prevent them from repeating the mistake. A good employee will not be satisfied with the mistake and strive to prevent it from happening again. A good manager will recognize what they are doing, support their efforts, and move forward rather than belaboring the point. Once the employee has the opportunity to prove they have learned from the earlier mistake, management should celebrate the success in some fashion and know that the employee is now an even greater asset to the organization. You should always look for ways to celebrate the employee's success with the employee. After all, it is theirs.

Never feel guilty for what you have earned.
Feel grateful for having had the opportunity to earn it.

Success can only be enjoyed if it comes through honesty and hard work. If success comes, be grateful for the opportunities and those who gave them to you. Be worthy of your successes and "give back" by providing opportunities to others. Remember that success is often a short-term situation. And once you achieve it, you must immediately begin striving toward your next success. Success can create momentum and, ultimately, cause more success. But you can quickly lose that momentum if you don't appreciate how you achieved it in the first place.

Overestimating can be as bad as underestimating.

At some point in time, you will be expected to provide an estimate on something. Whether it is time, resources, or an outcome, you will need to be as accurate as possible with your estimate. No one ever wants to underestimate a value and then have to determine how they will make up the difference once the actual value is determined. Inexperienced estimators may lack the confidence to be extremely accurate, and they will purposely inflate their estimate. They will "pad the numbers" so they are "covered". It is important to remember that estimating is normally required as part of a proposal of some type, and there are likely to be competing proposals. The downside of overestimating is that it may be done to a point that it is no longer competitive and the competition is lost. By overestimating, the estimator may lose the project and never have the opportunity to make up the difference like they would if they had underestimated. You must decide how fine a point you want to sharpen your pencil to and the risks in either doing it or not.

The "bottom line" may be your "top priority"
despite where it's located on the page.

Unless they are a nonprofit organization, organizations are in business to earn a profit. Simply put, profit is what remains when you subtract the total cost of operating an organization from the amount of incoming revenue. This fact applies whether you are operating a newspaper route or a megacorporation with countless employees. You must know your operating cost to determine what your minimum revenue must be to earn a profit. On the operations side of the organization, you will be expected to "watch cost", "cut cost", "reduce cost", "prevent cost", and any other directive required to maximize profits. On the sales and marketing side of the organization, you will be expected to "increase revenue", "generate revenue", "improve revenue", and any other directive required to maximize profits. Regardless of your position or level of responsibilities, your priority should be to do your very best to ensure your success and the success of your organization. That success is reflected in the bottom line. This is not greed. It's business. And it's your survival.

The devil does not need an advocate.

There are pros and cons to nearly everything. You should always approach issues considering that there are multiple perspectives. When offered a point, provide a counterpoint. Speak up at meetings if you have something to say. You can criticize a topic without attacking the messenger. You can point out flaws and offer alternative solutions, but never be the "devil's advocate". A wise woman once told me that the devil doesn't need one or deserve one.

To the victor go the spoils.
At least that's what they announced.

At some point in time, you may be part of a buyout, merger, or acquisition. These generally occur in the name of competition and trying to gain a competitive advantage. Despite what the press release may say, and even in the case of a merger, these rarely result in an equal partnership among the parties involved. There are countless scenarios that result in the combining of one or more organizations. It's not always one organization taking over another. Consider why multiple companies in the same market combine "horizontally". Is it to increase the overall market share and to gain advantages by the combination of their resources? Is it for one of them to rid itself of a competitor, or is it a combination of any of the above? Consider why multiple companies not within the same market end up under the same organizational banner. What is the advantage of doing so? Do their individual businesses complement each other such that the strength of them combined is greater than the sum of their individual strengths? This may be the case when a supplier and buyer formalize their relationship and join forces. If so, this type of "vertical" alignment may result in an improved situation for both. The challenge for you is to know the true reason for the buyout, merger, or acquisition, the direction of the newly-formed organization, and how it all impacts you as an employee regardless of your level of responsibility.

Who wants to work overtime?

Employees, for the most part, are paid in two specifically different manners: either by time or by task. Employees paid based on the amount of time they work are typically referred to as "hourly" employees since their rate of pay is normally referred to as a given amount per hour. There are two types of employees that are paid by task: the "commission" employee and the "salaried" employee. The employee that works on commission is normally paid a commission based upon the successful completion of a task. These are generally found in the sales department and their commission will either be a preestablished amount or a preestablished percentage of the sale that occurred. In many cases they will not receive any payment until the sale is completed. A salaried employee will be paid an amount that is based on the assigned task with successful completion not necessarily required for payment but probably required for continued employment. There are strict laws that dictate at what point the hourly rate increases for hourly employees. Unlike the hourly employee, employees working for commission or salary do not see their pay directly increase simply by working extra hours. Management will determine which one (or combination of the above compensation packages) they are willing to offer. They may pay extra for hourly employees to work overtime, or they may reduce their hours to reduce costs. They may place requirements on salaried employees that require them to work extra hours without any additional pay. They may offer bonuses and other financial incentives in both cases. You must know how much you are being paid, how you are being paid, and what that pay is based on. As a manager you must know how your employees are to be paid and how you can best leverage their time and abilities for you to be successful.

It's hard to miss it if you never had it.

Unless you plan to work until your dying day, you must plan for a time when you are not working and are not receiving a paycheck. Do not expect someone else to financially support you when that day comes, and never plan to rely on the government to do it. It's not their job, it's yours. There are countless individuals who are willing to offer you advice on how to plan for retirement, and some of them are actually qualified to do so. The plans are almost as numerous as the people suggesting the plans. My advice is free and it is very simple. Do not hesitate or procrastinate. Start saving on day one and continue contributing to your savings until your last day. If you begin setting aside a portion of your income the moment you receive it, you will never miss it. The longer you wait, the more accustomed you will be to receiving it. Setting it aside becomes more and more difficult. If you haven't started this practice yet, start now. Either invest your money or find someone to invest your money in areas that you are comfortable with and that reflect positively on you. It's your money. What is it doing for you, and what is it saying about you?

Ten important things to remember about interviewing.

1. Do not be late.
2. Dress better than the position requires.
3. Spit out your gum or candy before you meet the interviewer.
4. Minimize the amount of jewelry you wear. Wear a ring if you're married and always wear a watch.
5. Leave all mobile devices behind.
6. Use perfect posture and look the interviewer in the eye.
7. Try not to sit where you will be distracted. Interviewers like to go to restaurants and sit in front of a television to see how easily you are distracted.
8. Keep track and answer every question. An interviewer will ask you a question that requires a lengthy answer and then interrupt your response with quick questions that require short immediate answers. This is intended to interrupt and determine if you can keep your train of thought. Answer the short questions as they come, but always remember to go back and finish providing the original lengthy answer.
9. If the interview is scheduled along with a meal, order small portions. Eating is not your top priority, the interview is. If you're still hungry, you can eat afterwards.
10. Never drink alcohol during an interview. It doesn't matter if the interviewer offers or even if they are drinking, politely decline. Having a drink is not your top priority, the interview is. Once you land the job you can celebrate with a drink later if you're so inclined.

Ten important things I wish I'd known before I began business travel.

1. Make a note of where you leave your car at the airport.
2. Wear clothes that are easily removed at security.
3. Allow plenty of time and be prepared for delays.
4. Schedule yourself on early flights since flights tend to get delayed as the day wears on.
5. Keep your most essential items in your possession.
6. Make sure all your electronic devices are charged before embarking.
7. Keep all receipts in the same consistent location for future retrieval.
8. Be aware of your surroundings. Business travelers are easily recognized by the bad guys.
9. Never lay on the hotel bed before pulling the bedspread back. They may wash the sheets, but they do not wash the bedspreads.
10. Check the weather reports before you leave for your destination and pack accordingly.
11. Bonus tip: Allow time to pee before you get on the plane because they won't let you until you reach 10,000 ft. elevation. If you get delayed on the tarmac, you're NOT getting out of that seat.
12. Extra bonus tip: Don't hesitate requesting a different hotel room if the one next to yours has police tape on the door. You may even want to find a different hotel.
13. Extra extra bonus tip: Never ever, for the love of all that is good, sit next to a 13-year-old-first-time flier who filled up on Red Bull and Ding Dongs immediately before he boarded the plane.

Do not confuse a compromise with a win-win situation.

When two parties come together to form an agreement, both have their own demands, goals, expectations, aspirations, etc. Occasionally, everyone will get everything they want in the agreement, all goes well, and everyone wins. Unfortunately, this is not always possible and the agreement, when reached, is often the result of a compromise. A compromise is characterized by someone giving up something to someone in order to reach an agreement. Someone will not get everything they had originally planned for and thus fall short of a win. This is often the case and you should plan for it. If you plan to win, you can either limit your work to those areas where everyone CAN win, enter only into agreements with others who don't mind compromising, or you have to learn to negotiate. Good luck with the first two options. Here's how you do the third: Get all parties to modify their original plans. Determine what aspect of their plan is most important to them and ensure them that, at the minimum, they will get whatever it happens to be. If you can't ensure them they will get that part, move on to whatever they deem to be next in importance and determine if you can ensure they get it instead. Keep doing this until you find something you can guarantee them. Once you do, one party may give up one thing to get another while the other party may do the same. This process will go back and forth until both parties are respectively satisfied with the modifications to their original requests. They then have an agreement that everyone is satisfied with. Although it may not be the agreement that one or the other originally had in mind, that is soon forgotten if they are satisfied with the new agreement. You now have an agreement that everyone is satisfied with, everyone feels good about, and appears to be a win-win situation. This is not a compromise, it is called collaboration. It works very well as long as everyone is honest during the process. Otherwise, they will go back to their office and know they compromised. This will make collaboration more difficult the next time you get together but may not be your biggest concern if you are working with dishonest people.

There is no static state in business.
You are either moving forward or you're moving backwards.

Engineering schools require students to take a course called "Statics". This is an advanced physics course that deals with the relationship of forces that result in equilibrium between material objects. In short, you calculate forces and reactions based on their sum being zero, meaning that the objects receiving the forces do not move. There are no similar courses taught in business schools, with the possible exception of some accounting classes where the sum of all numbers must equal zero, but I will not mention those because they do not help serve to make my point. My point is that engineers like it when things are static and the wheels are not flying off in every direction. Business is different. Successful businesses must continue to evolve, change, and grow to remain successful. You can be sure their competition is striving to do the same. Business is a competitive business and your success is often measured in relation to the competition. If you are not moving forward, your competition will be and you will be moving backwards (in relationship to them). At this point, it is tempting to summarize by suggesting, "It's all relative." But that sounds a bit too much like something you hear in a physics class.

"Right size" for your business.

How large does your organization need to be? You must determine the requirements and establish the goals for your organization and then determine what size it needs to be. Never underestimate the importance of hiring an employee, the cost of a bad hire, and the benefits of retaining a good hire. New employees are expensive when you include all of the costs associated with recruiting, interviewing, hiring, and training. You must strive to find good applicants and then create a relationship and provide them the resources that will convert them into good employees. Once you have good employees, do whatever is practical to retain them. As they are retained they will become an even better employee if you establish a mutual set of expectations and then see them through. Once you have invested in a new employee, continue to monitor their progress. Employee retention is essential but only as it applies to good employees. There is no advantage to retaining poor employees, and when the day comes that you decide to part ways with an employee you must be fair to both you and them. Whereas recruiting, hiring, and training new employees is very expensive, the cost of reducing your staff can be even more expensive if not done properly.

Don't wait to "find" time to do the things you want to do.
"Make" time to do them.

At the onset of my freshman year of college, a professor told the class that we would not find time to do anything but study if we expected to succeed. If we wanted to do something else, we would need to make time to do it. Simply put, he was telling us to take control of our own outcome, don't expect things to just happen randomly, set our own priorities, and take responsibilities for the results.

Who are "They"?

I once knew a man who began every conversation by saying, "Well, you know, they tell me…" He never said who "they" were, and no one ever asked. "They" seemed to know everything about everything and everyone and yet no one ever asked who "they" were. Everyone just assumed that "they" were in the know and were above question. This was obvious by the reaction his statement received. Some people dropped what they were doing and immediately changed their course of action while others froze in their tracks and wasted time worrying how "they" knew so much and how what "they" knew would impact them. But still, no one dared question who "they" were and, consequently, never questioned the man delivering the news. The man was eventually accepted as the expert on all things important since "they" were always telling him what "they" knew. But who are "they" and who is he who quotes them? The reality was that "they" never existed but this comment allowed the man to present an idea, pass gossip, or make an accusation and then claim he was only the messenger if he was met with any resistance. Pronouns can be tricky things and people use them far too recklessly. Never be afraid to ask who "they" are.

Don't find yourself guilty by association.

There will be one person in the office that will be quick to give you credit for things you have done. This person will make a habit of "giving credit where credit is due". This sounds very good on the surface; however, you should exercise caution in accepting a pat on your back. This person will eventually give you credit for things you have had no involvement in. That is when it gets tricky. They might innocently do it by mistake, or they might be playing a very old game. In the latter case, your name will be automatically connected with something that it shouldn't and this isn't always good. People will hear it enough times that they will believe it. Make a point to correct the compliment before it goes too far. Take responsibility and accept credit for your actions and only your actions. You are not a loser just because "your team lost this past weekend", particularly if you're just a fan and don't even play for "your team".

Be careful what you ask for.
Be careful what you're asked for!

The boss will come to you and ask your opinion about something. Stop. Think. Proceed with caution. Ask yourself, "Is the boss looking for my opinion or my buy-in?" I once had a boss that would ask my opinion on a direction that he had already decided to take. I gave my opinion not knowing that it conflicted with a decision he had already arrived with. He wanted my opinion but not my input. He wanted to know where I stood on the topic. Good management will listen to an invaluable employee and rely on them as a subject-matter expert. As an employee you need to recognize what your boss is really looking for. As a manager, you don't need to play games with your employees to be a leader. Recognize who can provide invaluable input and ask for it before you make your decisions. Then engage all of the employees. If they are involved, they will own the decision.

Does the size of the office count?

Once an organization grows beyond two people, a hierarchy will exist. It may not be formal. It may not be complex. Everyone may not agree with it, but one will exist and questions of authority will follow. Some individuals will collaborate for the betterment of the organization while others will conspire for influence. These maneuvers will not be limited to individuals but will occur at the department and divisional levels also. Good management will clearly outline responsibilities and authority. The curious thing is how power and influence are measured by individuals who spend too much time prioritizing them without having the authority of assigning them. No one will measure the quality of work coming out of your office by the number of square feet that is in it. This being said, I've heard a few interesting attempts over the years.

"My office is bigger than yours."
"My office is closer to the president's than yours."
"I'm not about to give up office space to accounting. My department is the largest in the organization, just count the ceiling tiles if you don't believe me."
"I have an office with walls and a door. You're still in a cubicle."
"We must spend everything in our budget this year or management will reduce it next year and we don't want our budget cut. We worked hard to have the biggest budget in the organization and we need to stay #1!"
"We must act quickly to replace the employee that resigned yesterday before management decides we can survive without him. We worked hard to have the largest department in the organization and we need to stay #1!"
"The division located nearest to corporate headquarters will get preferential treatment."
"My office has a window."
"Oh, yea, I have a corner office."
"Ha!!! I have a corner office with windows, and it's bigger than both of yours combined. Just count the ceiling tiles if you don't believe me."

Know how to differentiate a salesmen and a deliverymen.

Imagine yourself in a business in need of a reliable janitorial department. Two individuals are vying for control of the custodial services department you depend on to maintain your operations. Both individuals approach you with the same proposal. While one has a slick presentation, quoting great people and using technical terminology you don't understand, the other stumbles through a prepared presentation leaving you bored and nearly asleep. You are going to lean towards the one that wowed you. No one can blame you for that. Before the project is delivered it has gone over budget and past schedule. Once delivered, you learn that the scope is not nearly what you had been led to believe it was. Not by coincidence, the individual from custodial services who sold you on the project is already busy pitching his next proposal before this project is delivered. He has moved on because, as he explains, he is a forward-thinking person. You are tempted to focus on "the next big thing" because technology is moving forward at a rapid pace. Additionally, the next project sounds so good that you will be tempted to accept lackluster results from the last one in order to move on to the next one. This cycle will repeat itself as long as you allow it to. Meanwhile, the second individual from custodial services is proceeding along under the radar, finishing smaller less flashy projects and delivering results. The first individual can sell any idea that comes along but never seems to be able to deliver. The second one can deliver but will never get the opportunity to. Which one do you really need? That's a trick question. You need both. Identify who the salesmen and the deliverymen are. Let the salesmen sell and the deliverymen deliver regardless of whether they work in custodial services or any other department. You just have to realize who is who and which is which and never let one convince you that he is the other.

Every kickoff party deserves a wrap party.

Organizations recognize change doesn't come easy and will go to great lengths to get their employees to embrace something new. One of the most common ways to start a new project, initiative, or sales program is to hold a "kickoff" party. They do this because it works. Employees will respond positively if they are convinced that the project, etc., is beneficial. Once the employees are inspired, it is management's responsibility to ensure that the project is completed and the desired results are accomplished. It is at this point that many organizations fail to complete the full circle by hosting a "wrap" party. Everyone enjoys a certain level of closure, and as a manager you must plan to include a party offering them the opportunity to have closure. You owe it to those employees who you hosted at the onset.

Unfortunately, there are organizations, departments, and individuals that are very good at throwing parties to start a project but never seem to have a party to celebrate its successful completion. Take a hard look at this and consider whether they simply don't celebrate or, just as likely, they never completed the project. There are two notable downsides to this. First, the organization never finishes anything they started and, secondly, the employees will recognize this and become increasingly cynical about the next "big thing" that management wants them to get excited about. This increases the challenge in getting everyone motivated. But never fear, they'll just plan a larger party next time.

What value do you add?

Regardless of what you do, you need to contribute. You need to add value to whatever it is you are contributing to. Those receiving your contribution must recognize what you contribute, and as long as they place more value on your contribution than you do, you will enjoy a certain level of success. Your level of success will increase as the value they place on your contribution increases. This applies to every aspect of life and is not limited to your professional career. For that reason, you should never underestimate its importance. Furthermore, you should continually reassess the value of your contribution and determine ways you can increase it. Review everything you do during the course of your day and apply one simple litmus test: "Does this add value?" If it doesn't, discontinue doing it. If it does, work at it in such a way that you maximize the value it adds.

Let's do lunch.

It's all about being honest and sincere. Run into an old business acquaintance that you've not seen or talked to in years. Have a nice conversation and smile when they say the two of you "really need to get together sometime". If they really felt this way, why has it been so long since the two of you visited? If YOU feel this way, what have you been waiting for? Set your priorities. If you want to have lunch with someone, ask them, and then schedule it. Do not waste your time giving it lip service because it sounds like something that needs to be said. Do it. If you do not expect to have lunch, don't suggest it. Otherwise, you risk becoming insincere and eventually losing your integrity. Rather than saying "Let's do lunch!" ask them, "Would you like to have lunch?" If they say, "Yes," then ask them, "When are you available?" Keep putting the ball in their court and you'll find whether they really want to get together sometime. It'll become obvious if they keep putting you off. Recognize it, don't worry about it, and move on. If they suggest lunch, put the ball right back into their court and say, "Yes. When would you like to get together?" If they're sincere, they'll suggest a date. If they're not, you'll know it and so will they. Recognize it, don't worry about it, and move on. Lunch is overrated anyway. Breakfast is the most important meal of the day.

Scheduling is like completing a jigsaw puzzle.

Nothing lasts forever. Consequently, everything has a start point and an end point. Each thing's schedule is defined by its relationship to everything else with a start point and end point. Every aspect of business has a schedule, and every schedule is as unique as that which is being scheduled. Schedules apply not just to people; they are set for all resources, tasks, and projects. As a result, efficient scheduling is critical to business success and, in some cases, is an art form. The items going into a schedule vary widely. Characteristics such as capabilities, requirements, availability, predictability, and size all cause the items going into a schedule to vary. The scheduler must take all of these into account when developing a schedule and creating the required result. The key to scheduling is taking input of all shapes and sizes and fitting them together so every piece is optimally utilized and every void is filled. Think of it like a giant puzzle.

Be aware of round numbers.

While there are twenty six letters in the alphabet, there are only ten digits in our counting system. For this reason alone, I have always thought math should be easier than spelling. I am sure many people would disagree. Computer programing must be incredibly simple since computers only require two digits (1's and 0's). I am sure many people would disagree. Likewise, accounting must be easier than engineering since accountants only take numbers to two places past the decimal point while engineers often work with numbers carried out to four or more places past the decimal point. I am sure many people would disagree, especially accountants. With regard to numbers, there is a one in ten (10%) chance that a number will end with a zero. Similarly, there is a one in one hundred (1%) chance that a number will end with two zeroes, a one in one thousand (0.1%) chance it will end in three zeroes and so on. As numbers get larger, businesses that deal in them tend to round them off. There is nothing wrong with rounding the numbers off, but question individuals who claim to provide you an "exact", "accurate", "thoroughly-calculated", "precise" value that ends in zeroes. The more zeroes, the increased chances it's an estimate. If it's an estimate, you have a better chance of negotiating it to a value that is more in your favor. Calculate your chances to make the best decision. Just don't round off the number to zero.

Repeat customers are important.

The experts all agree that repeat customers are one of the main components to a successful business; that's why they are experts, because they are right. You must recognize this and do everything you can to keep repeat customers, but don't confuse "repeat" with "permanent". There is no such thing as a permanent customer, and you have to be prepared to replace the repeat customers when they are no longer there regardless of who is responsible for them no longer being there. You have to continually find, recruit, and service new customers. Today's new customer is tomorrow's repeat customers, and repeat customers are one of the main components to a successful business. Any expert will tell you that.

What are there dashed lines on an organizational chart?

Most organizations will use an organizational chart to graphically illustrate its reporting structure. Each employee's name is placed in a box with a solid line connecting it to a box containing the supervisor's name. That box may have numerous lines leading to it depending on how many people the supervisor is supervising. The box containing the supervisor's name will have a solid line connecting it to a box containing the supervisor's supervisor's name and so on. Supervisors are usually listed above employees, so as you move up the corporate ladder, your name moves up the org chart. This is all well laid out and easy to follow until someone in management starts suggesting dashed lines to accompany the solid lines. What do the dashed lines represent, why are they needed, and how do they impact you?

Dashed lines are intended to represent secondary responsibilities in the case that an employee must report on specific responsibilities to more than one individual. In those cases, a dashed line will connect the employee's name with the secondary supervisor. This works fine if, and only if, the employee and the supervisors all understand and agree to the reporting structure and who is responsible for reporting what to whom. Unfortunately, this is not always the case. More often, dashed lines result in confusion when the supervisors do not agree on the employee's responsibilities and their own roles. Imagine how the employee feels about this and the resulting lack of direction having to "serve two masters". Good management will recognize the conflict and resolve it. Poor management will not. Know your place in the organization, your responsibilities, and who you're responsible to. And remember, the name in the box at the top of the organizational chart probably still reports to someone somewhere but has a whole lot more say-so pertaining to the boxes and lines on the chart. The further you move up the chart, the closer you are to that box.

Don't read your presentation.

Communication is essential. Most business surveys I have taken identify "lack of communication" as a primary problem in business. Technology has not helped and, quite possibly, may have made the situation worse. I agree with this but not because technology is useless. It is not useless, it is only misused.

You will eventually be required to make some type of presentation as part of your responsibilities to communicate something to somebody or somebodies. At some point in history, putting words on paper was considered high tech. You shouldn't underestimate this proven form of communication. Make yourself notes and provide handouts, but only as a communication aid. There was a time in the more recent past that chalkboards, whiteboards, and overhead projectors were considered high tech. Use them as necessary but only as an aid. With the introduction of digital communication, the opportunities are nearly without end, but so are the chances for misuse. Use them as necessary, but only as an aid. Only as an aid! There's only thing worse than someone providing a page of notes to supplement their presentation and then reading line after line from the notes. It's the modern day equivalent. Do not provide some type of visual digital presentation to your audience and then proceed to read directly from it. Your audience is there to listen to you speak. They are not there to watch and listen to you read. Use technology to supplement your presentation and then present your presentation. Do not read it.

Call "Can't" busters.

Why is it so easy to be negative when there's so much to gain by being positive? It seems that being negative is often easier than being positive, but this defies a couple laws of physics so I don't buy it. Instead, I believe we have made it easier to be negative and much of that ease can be found in the words we use. "No" is easier to say than "yes". It takes less effort, trust me. I would suggest you try it, but my intent of this is to encourage you to be positive, and suggesting you say "No" would be counterproductive.

We have the word "not" that we apply to most positive actions to make them negative. We easily change "can" to "cannot", "will" to "will not", "did" to "did not", and others such as "shall", "have", "has", and "had". We have even taken steps to make this even easier by contracting these words to "can't", "won't", "didn't", "shan't", "haven't", "hasn't" and "hadn't". How convenient is that? It can be a challenge to encourage others to be positive. Use positive language when you are communicating with your employees, coworkers, and supervisors.

I once made a proposal to a group and expected to receive a negative response. I asked for their input and tried to keep count of the number of times they said the word "can't". I lost count in less than two minutes. After they finished pointing out every reason under the sun why they couldn't support the proposal (although they liked it), I wrote the word "CAN'T" in big bold letters and then circled it and placed a line through the circle.

I called it "Can't Busters". I laid it on the table and told them, "Don't tell me why we can't do something we agree needs to be done. Tell me what we CAN and MUST do to make it happen." They were still tempted to say, "Can't," and every time they did, I pointed at the sheet of paper. It took a while and a lot of hard work, but I finally busted the habit. That team became one of the most positive, innovative groups I have ever worked with and eventually realized its own potential.

Unless you are a meteorologist,
the conversation is over when it turns to the weather
(unless you live in Oklahoma where it is the only topic of
conversation).

Communication is one of the keys to success. You have to know how to communicate. You must be able to start a conversation, maintain it, and know when it is over. There's a point in every conversation when it is no longer being productive. Don't waste your time gossiping, it benefits no one. And whether you know it or not, good management knows who's gossiping in the organization. Spend your time being creative and discuss ideas that will contribute to your success and the success of your organization. Focus your attention on productive issues and stay focused. Work your way through the "awkward pauses" and recognize that the conversation is no longer productive once it turns to topics that are completely out of your control. The most common is the weather. There are times when you need to discuss the weather. You need to know if it will impact the business, employee welfare, and customer satisfaction. But idle chitchat about the weather is useless. You can't do anything about it, so don't let it ruin an otherwise productive conversation. You might as well be discussing the fact the sun will rise in the east tomorrow morning.

If that's the worst thing that happens to us today, we'll do just fine.

Put it into perspective. Is it really worth worrying about? Could it have been a lot worse? Probably so.
Not everything will go right. Not everything will go the way you want or expect it to. That's true in life as well as in business. Deal with it. Deal with it and move on. Change your plans, adjust your schedule, make accommodations, and simply deal with what comes your way. Do what is necessary, don't overreact, make informed decisions to address whatever comes your way regardless of how good or bad it is. Once you have done this, you can move on, and once you look back you'll recognize that most things weren't as bad as they seemed at the time. Once you have moved on, if you're able to look back at it, it could have been worse. Try reminding yourself of this while you're dealing with those little things that come your way and you'll find they're easier to deal with.

It's a "system"!

There are few words I have heard used more in business operations than "system". Ironically, the more it is used the more it defies explanation. It seems to apply to everything but define nothing. You can "work the system", "buck the system", or "be a part of the system". There are "system programmers" and there are "system analysts". There's a "financial system", "an operational system", "an electrical system", "a mechanical system" and the all-important "engineering system". Ask any engineer. There's also the one that no one wants to discuss: "the failed system". I have listened to lecturers use this term as if it labeling something a "system" made the mundane more special. It doesn't. Anytime two or more functional operations function together, they are a "system". It's as simple as that. It is normally what is expected since few functional operations are intended to work alone and often fail when they do. Combine your functional operations together in such a way that they create a system. Get your system to work so smoothly that it appears to be a single functional operation. Then combine what now appears to be a single functional operation with other functional operations. Get them to work together in such a way that they create a system capable of greater achievement and success. Continue this process and continue your success, but don't ever hesitate calling it a "system" at any point in the process since it will ultimately sound much more impressive when you do.

Team vs. Silo

There may be no "I" in team, but there is in silo. Coincidence? Maybe not. Managers like to discuss the benefits of teamwork, but then operate their functions as individual silos with separate and often competing goals. There is no "one size fits all" as it pertains to organizational structure and responsibilities. There are pros and cons to establishing teams as well as silos. Managers need to know which approach is optimal while employees need to know which is being used. A team of employees will enjoy success when everyone on the team knows and accepts their individual responsibilities and all work together to fulfill the responsibility of the team. The team will enjoy additional success if the members of the team can fulfill more than one responsibility. That's where cross-training becomes beneficial. Likewise, an organization of silos will be successful if everyone knows and accepts their individual responsibilities and adequately communicates them among the silos. Cross-training is not necessary and employees have the opportunity to become high-performing specialists at what they do. However, they do this at the cost of not being able to multitask and limiting their potential growth. Each approach has its place. It is management's responsibility to know when and where to implement one, the other, or a combination of both.

Set a goal and then
schedule backwards rather than schedule forward.

Have you ever set a goal that you never accomplished? Did you wonder why it was not accomplished? Did you review your plan to accomplish it? Did you have a plan? If so, how did you schedule your plan?

They say, "You have to walk before you can run." That is true, but when do you plan on walking? Take a different approach to this and say, "You can't run until you learn to walk," and there seems to be a greater urgency on learning to walk. If you plan to increase the length of your daily jog until you run a marathon, what is the incentive to run further tomorrow? What are the chances you'll ever cross that finish line?

If you set a goal to run a marathon by the end of the year, determine how far you need to be running by the end of September. If you have to be running that distance by the end of September, how far must you be running by the end of June? If you have to be running that distance by the end of June, how far must you be running by the end of March? Obviously, if you have to be running that distance by the end of March, how far must you be running at the beginning of the year. Assuming today is January 1 and you know how far you can run, you should know if you have even a remote chance of running a marathon this time next year. If you can't meet today's requirement, why do you think you can meet your year-end goal? You need to rethink your goal, rethink your schedule, or start bicycling.

Schedule your professional goals this way, whether they are personal or organizational, and you'll increase your chances of accomplishing them.

Are you working while at "work"?

The key to true lasting success is found in honest hard work. Don't expect to receive anything without giving something in return. Don't accept anything free since you can never fully appreciate something unless you earned it. Whether you're an employee or the CEO, do not be late for work. And once you get there, earn what you are receiving by putting in an honest day's work. But what is an honest day's work? What are you being paid to do? What are you paying your employees to do? Are you doing it? Are they?

There's a reason why some employees record "billable hours" by tracking, sometimes down to the minute, exactly what they do and then charge for only the time specifically assigned to the task. This is far more exact than punching a time clock at the beginning and the end of each day recording how many hours you were at work.

Are you working every minute of every hour you are at work? Consider all of the downtime a person has while at work. Some of it is acceptable and some is not. Some is questionable while some may be provided and allowed by law. In the simplest example, you and your employees will not work eight hours during an eight-hour shift once you include smoke breaks, coffee breaks, lunch breaks, water breaks, rest breaks, and downtime every time the computer system breaks. These are all to be expected, especially the computer breakage. You must account for them when you plan, schedule, and budget regardless of what level of organization you work in.

Problem/Challenge/Opportunity

You will have setbacks. Things will go wrong and will go wrong when you least expect them to. How will you respond to them? The pessimist will view them as a problem. The cautious optimist may view them as a challenge. The true optimist will view them as an opportunity. Take the opportunity to make every setback an opportunity and you'll never run out of opportunities.

I am "unbelievable"!

When an associate approaches you and asks, "How are you, today?" Try replying, "Unbelievable." Do this particularly if you are having a lousy day. Always be positive. And rather than sharing a negative mood, use, "Unbelievable," as a safe alternative. You won't be lying, especially if you are having an unbelievably lousy day. Additionally, you won't be lying if you are having an unbelievably great day. Regardless of how your day is, you are unbelievable. And the truth is since your associate has not lived your day it may be difficult for them to fully understand the specific details of how you are and unable to believe them if you shared them. So once again, you'd be unbelievable. The amazing thing about replying, "Unbelievable," is that most people will immediately assume it's a good thing. It's as if being good is much more unbelievable than being bad. Whether you intend to or not, you are sounding positive, and in some cases unbelievably positive whether YOU believe it or not. So simply reply, "Unbelievable." Because replying, "You wouldn't believe me if I told you," might seem a bit rude, albeit truthful.

Relieve the bottleneck.

Every process has a limit. Whether you are sitting customers at a restaurant, pumping water through a pipeline, making widgets, or getting commuters from point A to point B, there is only so much that can be processed. Since most processes consist of a series of steps, tasks, or stages, the limiting factor of the overall process will be found in one of those parts. The limiting part of the overall capacity is your bottleneck. It is the factor, or factors, that is preventing you from doing more. So what do you do with it?
A chain is only as strong as its weakest link and a team is only as strong as its weakest member. Once again, the experts are right. That's why they're the experts. It's a shame they can't get everyone to listen to them and believe what they say. But then again, if the experts were to develop that expertise, they would eventually land a higher paying job writing articles in celebrity gossip magazines. I digress.
Once you determine what the bottleneck is, determine how to relieve it, determine what the impact will be, and determine if it is worth addressing. If you gain nothing by relieving it, it may have not been the bottleneck. Organizations make investments they hope will result in growth, however, growth may never be realized if the investment is not made in the right areas. Why increase your salesforce if you can't manufacture what you're already selling? Why increase your fabrication capability if you can't sell enough to keep your factories running today? You may be taking steps for long term future growth, but those should be balanced with the steps you need take today. You can address a bottleneck numerous ways including adding staff, overtime, machinery, or a third lane. These may be quick, direct, and easy, but all of these add costs as well.
Consider relieving the bottleneck by first making process improvements. Increase throughput, reduce downtime, provide training, and eliminate errors. These are not as easy to identify. They may not be as glamorous or as easy to implement, but they will generally be less expensive and prove more effective in the long run. When you do this, do not be surprised if you still have a bottleneck. You will always have a bottleneck. You can never eliminate it. You can only relieve it or move it to a new location. You have succeeded as long as the new bottleneck, regardless of where it is, is less restrictive than the old one.

How flexible are you?

Businesses must have income to stay in business. Even nonprofit organizations must have some type of income to offset the cost of operating. Operational costs require organizations to spend money. Some of that spend reoccurs on a regular basis, varies only slightly, and is referred to as a "fixed cost" or "fixed spend". Items such as utilities, rent, taxes, and overhead all fall into this category. "Flexible spend" is money spent on items that vary along with the variations in your organizational needs. It is important to recognize what types of cost are fixed and what types are flexible. Once you can account for your "fixed costs", you can manage and adjust your "flexible spend" to maximize its benefit and your success.

In the simplest example, an employee's salary is a "fixed cost" if the employee is filling a permanent position. Management can add employees if business picks up, but cannot consider them permanent unless it expects to maintain business at the new heightened levels. If management recognizes that the additional business is only temporary, it can consider adding part-time or temporary employees but must also consider the associated fixed costs such as training the new employees. To prevent incurring these costs, management may opt to offer permanent employees overtime pay or other incentives. As a manager, offer an employee additional compensation to work more but never pay them to work harder. This would indicate you are currently paying them to work at a level less than their capabilities. Did you hire them to give you 90% effort? As an employee, recognize what is fixed and what is flexible. Take advantage of any opportunity to fill the "flexible spend" that your organization is offering. It may require you to work more but it will send the right message to management. The key here is to be flexible.

Do not confuse sympathy with empathy.

If you make an error, take responsibility and correct it. Correct it as quickly as reasonable and practical. Apologize if an apology is required as part of the correction. Do not apologize for someone else's error. You might be able to correct it, but no matter how bad you feel about the error or how bad you feel for the person receiving the error, do not apologize for someone else's mistake. Your apology is not, and cannot be, sincere if you are not responsible for the error. Do not confuse being sympathetic with being empathetic. Place yourself in their shoes. Understand what they are dealing with and the impact the mistake has had on them. Once you do, you can better relate to them and be truly sincere with your words and actions. This is often more difficult and takes more effort but that is why it is more likely to translate into sincerity. No one can expect you to be perfect. You're not. No one is. But by being empathetic, by placing yourself in someone else's shoes, you'll understand the impact of your decisions and learn to make better ones. You'll understand your customers and have better ones. You'll understand your coworkers and be a better one. It is not always easy, but the important things are often more difficult to achieve. And in the case that you are completely unable to be empathetic to others, then you really have something to apologize for.

Messengers should wear bullet proof vests.

People find it difficult to separate the message from the messenger. If you're going to be a messenger, you will need to do it for them.

The person with the problem most likely has the solution.

Coworkers, employees, and even bosses may choose to approach you requesting your feedback or input. Don't feel burdened if their requests are sincere. Feel flattered that they value your input enough to ask for it. What do you do once you hear them out? Regardless of whether you have input, the entire solution, or are completely clueless, there is one simple fact you must not overlook. There's a very good possibility that they know the problem much better than you do since you may have just learned of it when they brought it to you. Hopefully, they gave it some tangible amount of thought before bringing it to you and are therefore more familiar with it than you are. The more familiar they are with the problem, the more likely they are to have already considered a solution. So do not hesitate to ask them if they already have one. It may require effort, but once you provide some coaxing and encouragement, do not be surprised if they can provide their own solution. If they do, it is your opportunity to collaborate with them to determine if their solution is the best solution. It may be. It may not be. If it isn't, continue the collaboration until both of you agree what is.
Not everyone will participate. There will be those who just want you to solve their problems for them. Others just want to complain and do not expect you to provide any type of input, feedback, or solution. The key is to determine which ones want to collaborate and which ones just want to whine.

Choose a chair of your choosing.

Meetings are one of the most dynamic aspects of business, particularly those that include conflict. I've been in mediation meetings where the parties sat on opposite sides of the room, faced each other, and "mediated" until the last man standing won the day in a daylong battle that would make Napoleon pull his hand out of his lapel and erupt into a spontaneous applause in a way only a guy who has been dead for 200 years could. The lines were drawn, the lieutenants were in place, the scouts had returned with reports from their reconnaissance outings, and the battle began. This type of meeting may be necessary if the parties involved are actually competing for the same prize. But I have seen this type of behavior between groups within the same organization that should have been focused on their mutual success.
I've been in less hostile meetings where the participants still tended to congregate in smaller groups. These groups all brought their own specific set of interests, goals, and agendas. This often resulted in conflict that was unnecessary, counterproductive, and conflict that probably wouldn't have existed had the seating arrangement been more homogeneous.
Consider this when hosting a meeting: assign seating if necessary, and as necessary, to achieve the goals you have for your meeting. If you are attending someone else's meeting, unless you are assigned a seat, choose one that helps you meet your own goals for the meeting. Try sitting among participants who you have nothing in common with. You may learn something new, your proximity may prevent a unnecessary conflict, and you may contribute to the meeting in a way that allows it to end sooner rather than later. After a few meetings you'll understand that this last benefit is everyone's goal in a meeting. In the case you do, you'll be hailed as a hero.
Just be cautious. If conflicts arise, you don't want to be too deep in enemy territory. You don't want to be perceived as a traitor. You don't want anyone to think you've changed your colors. Do not get caught wearing the enemy's uniform or you risk being shot by your own army for treason or hung as a spy by the enemy. I'm sure Napoleon would offer the same advice, although it might be in French.

Conflict resolution will begin the moment the questions begin.

Conflict will arise in every shape and form and when you least expect it but don't confuse conflict with argument. Conflict exists in most "whats", "whos", "whens", "hows" and "whys" every time more than one opinion or approach is presented. This doesn't mean an argument has to ensue and true professionals will not allow one to. What needs to be done? Who needs to do it? When does it need to be done? How does it need to be done? Why are we doing it in first place?

Just as most conflicts begin with a question, you should ask yourself a few questions before you proceed. Is it worth my time and effort to proceed? Do I need to proceed? Can I be successful if I proceed? What will I have to give up in order to proceed? Is the other person willing to proceed with me?

Most people who proceed into a conflict do so with purpose. The greater the purpose is, the greater the conflict will be. They know there is a conflict. They may have asked themselves enough questions to decide how they are going to proceed. But at that point, they move forward leaving the interrogatives behind and carrying only declarations along with them. They approach the resolution phase of the conflict with facts and demands because anything else will indicate signs of weakness. And they are not about to do that because they are determined to win.

I suggest approaching the resolution phase with questions. You will understand where you stand. You'll be better prepared to make your own decisions and you'll know what chance you have of collaborating together toward a win-win resolution. Once resolved, you can move on to your next conflict. There's bound to be another one in your near future.

Take a moment and find a "moment".

As a structural engineer, I have designed countless beams and columns. Years ago, I observed I was not much different than the beams I was designing. We both had to be able to span between support points without collapsing. We both had to resist forces that were not of our own making, and those forces resulted in fatigue, strain, and stress. I've always believed that if something is consistent, it is predictable. If it is predictable, it is dependable. If it is dependable, it can be managed. I understand that the forces we deal with are as unpredictable as the stress that results from them, so I sat down to calculate what type of force would result in a consistent stress on the entire length of a simple beam. Amazingly, the force is referred to in physics as a "moment", and as the other forces increase, the moment must be increased until it is so great that it evens out the amount of stress along the beam's length.
If I were to compare myself to the simple beam, I could use this analogy and find a "moment" so great it would even out all of my stresses and ultimately make them manageable.
If I consider myself as the beam, the distance between the supports to be the length of my day, and my wife to be the support at each end of my day, Courtney and Creighton, you provided the "moment" that leveled the stresses and ultimately made them manageable every time I returned from work, walked into the house, and heard, "Daddy's Home!"
Take a moment and find your "moment"!

CPSIA information can be obtained at www.ICGtesting.com
Printed in the USA
LVOW10s1052061215
465613LV00033B/970/P